LIFE
SIGNS

Claire Petulengro is the astrologer for *Metro*, the *Sunday People* and *Take It Easy* magazine, the *Mirror*'s *We Love Telly* magazine, *Company*, *Pick Me Up* and over a hundred regional newspapers. Her TV appearances have been seen by millions and range from *This Morning*, MTV, *The Big Breakfast*, *Richard and Judy* and *The Gloria Hunniford Show* to the ratings-topper *Predictions* with Philip Schofield and Kirsty Young. She also appears regularly on *The Steve Wright Show* and Sky's *Gala Bingo*. She was the resident astrologer at the Express Newspaper Group for over three years and at *OK!* for over five years.

Claire, who is of Romany heritage, is the daughter of famous celebrity astrologer Eva Petulengro and lives in Brighton with her four children.

You can find out more about Claire's current projects at www.clairepetulengro.com and www.clairepetulengro.co.uk.

ALSO BY CLAIRE PETULENGRO

Love Stars
Health Signs
Diet Signs

LIFE SIGNS

Let the power of the
stars guide you to success

CLAIRE PETULENGRO

PAN BOOKS

First published 2009 by Pan Books

This edition published 2010 by Pan Books
an imprint of Pan Macmillan, a division of Macmillan Publishers Limited
Pan Macmillan, 20 New Wharf Road, London N1 9RR
Basingstoke and Oxford
Associated companies throughout the world
www.panmacmillan.com

ISBN 978-0-330-46064-4

1 3 5 7 9 8 6 4 2

A CIP catalogue record for this book is available
from the British Library.

Printed and bound in the UK by
CPI Mackays, Chatham ME5 8TD

To Jonathan Nicholas Mark Ledgard, thank you for being an amazing husband and daddy and for remembering the colour of my eyes when my back was to you in China! I love you.

For Paris, Carmen Valentine, Lucy Victoria May and Honey, life is what you make it! Make yours count, my babies. Mummy xxx

ACKNOWLEDGEMENTS

Thank you to Ingrid Connell and my extended family at Pan Macmillan.

To my wonderful parents, especially my mother and mentor, Eva Petulengro, love and gratitude for teaching and nurturing me in astrology and everything else in life! Thanks also to my lovely uncle, Leo Petulengro, for his artwork.

Much love and respect goes to Vicki McIvor, for being the best literary agent I could ask for, while still being a great mum to the lovely Lara.

Gratitude to my agent, Sara Cameron, a brave woman to take on looking after someone like me and for all the adventures I know we will share along the way in the years to come. Thank you for what is sure to be a colourful journey.

It would be unthinkable not to say thank you as always to Melanie Cantor for a great beginning. I would not be where I am today if it were not for you and your Cancerian honesty.

And thanks to Gordon Wise, a great person and a wonderful friend, who first gave me my dream of writing books.

I am grateful to Elle and Mitchell Phillips from Studio 57, for their expert health and fitness advice. The best in their field!

And last but not least, this book would not have been possible if I didn't have a husband who does night feeds, school runs, nappies, washing-up and hoovering while still paying me compliments. Thank you, super daddy!

CONTENTS

Introduction

YOUR ELEMENTAL
LIFE PLAN

'As above so below.'

There are many self-help books available in this day and age. Indeed, most of us will have at least one, if not several, lurking somewhere in our homes or bags. Whether it's how to make a million, how to retire early or how to find true love, there's a subject covered that touches each and every one of our hearts. However, no other book has joined together the obvious link between our star sign and the pattern by which we live our lives. *Life Signs* is tailor-made with *your* sign in mind to help you find success where before you may have failed.

Working with clients from all walks of life and understanding the way that different star signs approach the hurdles of life has taught me a lot. I've seen that Pisceans are drawn openly to experiences that they know are going to hurt them, that Geminis always think the grass is greener on the other side of the fence and that Librans allow themselves to be emotionally manipulated time and time again. Over the years I have felt my role change from client to client. Sometimes I am like a priest, hearing confessions that the person I am seeing needs to get off their chest – that affair, that lie, that guilt. Sometimes I am like a best friend, someone who gives the client the support they need to take an important step forward in life. The roles vary but the problems are often the same: people are living life in the way they think others want them to do, rather than believing in themselves and valuing what they really want and what will make them happy.

My family are Romanies and have studied the human race for generations. Our Romany upbringing and heritage is all about people – their lives, their loves, their fears and their problems. In the past Romanies, being travellers, never went to school and weren't taught limitations. Quite the opposite – Romanies are taught to say what they feel. Giving readings is second nature to us, and as a child I would sit with my mother and grandmother when they were reading their clients' palms. I would be asked, 'Claire, what do you feel about this lady?' and I would say what I felt without hesitation, whether it was sadness at a recent loss, pain due to an illness or joy concerning a pregnancy. Children from a different background would have been more likely to answer what they knew they were supposed to be thinking and feeling rather than trusting their gut instinct.

My great-grandmother kept the secrets of the rich and famous. My grandmother knew whose children had fathers they would never meet and which wealthy faces didn't have a penny to their name. Sitting with my mother when she gave readings exposed me to a multitude of experiences before I was even twenty-one. By her side, I saw clients grow and change before my eyes. I also saw beliefs that had previously been set in stone melt away, like a snowflake in the sun. Illegitimate children were no longer a sin, unmarried couples were the norm, and sleeping together for fun was as acceptable as sharing condiments. While social values may have changed, human emotions have stayed the same; only now the influence of the internet, television, chat and reality shows and our increasing openness to analysis have made us more self-critical and aware than ever before.

So what will you find in these pages that can change and inspire you? We will analyze your love life, your needs and desires, your weaknesses and the rules you should follow to find success. Each sign has different weaknesses in relationships. Libra is far too easily emotionally manipulated, and Aries jumps in feet first before thinking of the consequences. It is usually only when baby number two comes along that Aries realizes that this should have been just a fling. Learn to recognize when you are being untrue to yourself and you can prevent these problems. I don't think that the divorce rate is higher because we've become more open-minded; I think we've become more narrow-minded as we increasingly judge ourselves on what our next-door neighbours are doing and what the glamorous magazines and A-list celebs are able to achieve. We set impossible dreams as targets instead of allowing ourselves to get what *we* want and need.

We will look at careers and what working environment best suits each sign, making sure your job can be something you enjoy and look forward to each day. If you feel sluggish in the morning (especially Aries, Cancerians and Pisceans), I'm going to give you back your energy and glow, and teach you the right foods for your sign to fuel your body.

Money can attract us to someone, but it can also tear us apart from the one we love. How many of you have lied to a partner or family member about what an item cost to avoid embarrassment? Geminis, Aquarians and Scorpios most certainly have, and Sagittarians and Leos don't do a bad job of fibbing over prices either. Let's tackle finances head on. There is no reason for you to feel you can't cope. I'm here to show you the most up-to-date ways to deal with money worries and to work on getting your bank balance out of the red and into the black. I've done it before for clients, and I can do it for you.

Are you living in the wrong surroundings to bring out

your true potential? I have tips on everything from where you should be holidaying to how you should style your home and what kind of parties you will like best.

It's hard to know the right thing to do in life at the best of times. We get over one obstacle only to discover another. Sometimes it can seem as if life is one big challenge with no breaks in sight. Working as an astrologer has enabled me to meet a range of people, from royalty to pop stars, politicians, doctors, lawyers, teachers, policemen, clergymen, shopworkers, showgirls and ladies of the night. An astrologer's job is not an easy one. We're supposed to have all of the answers. However, a good astrologer doesn't tell you what to do but helps you find the answers in your own heart, because when your crisis is over and you continue on your journey in life, you need to have the confidence to face the next hurdle on your own. We can't always have someone with us twenty-four seven. If we did, life would be pretty boring. I want to teach you how to have confidence in yourself and trust your instincts. By getting to know yourself better, you can learn your strengths.

You would be surprised how many people try to conform because they think that they will get laughed at if they trust in what they feel or if they have the confidence to take control of their destiny. We often say what we think other people want to hear because we don't want to seem different. I've been laughed at, believe me, but not since I left the playground. In fact I got an email only recently from one of my bullies who apologized for the hard time they had given me at school. It sort of came full circle for me, especially as she had been a non-believer in all things psychic and was asking for advice on the doctorate she was now taking ... on astrology and its relationship with modern medicine.

By reading *Life Signs* you will learn that we all have hurdles to overcome. You will learn how to be *you* – how to respect yourself, love yourself and learn to love your faults. Many of us are living out our parents' dreams or paying the price for their mistakes. It's time to break free from those restraints and I'm going to show you how. Let the new you begin and let a better life commence.

WORKING OUT
YOUR STAR SIGN

Here's a quick guide for those of you who don't already know your sign:

ARIES: The Ram
21 March to 20 April

Ruling planet: Mars, the Roman god of war
Triplicity or element: fire
Keywords: headstrong, opinionated, initiator, leader, loyal to a cause, egotistical, passionate
Lucky day: Tuesday

TAURUS: The Bull
21 April to 21 May

Ruling planet: Venus, the planet of love
Triplicity or element: earth
Keywords: stubborn, sensual, loyal, affectionate, materialistic, craves stability and security
Lucky day: Friday

GEMINI: The Twins
22 May to 21 June

Ruling planet: Mercury, the planet of communication
Triplicity or element: air
Keywords: generous, restless, adaptable, excitable, fickle, two-sided
Lucky day: Wednesday

 CANCER: The Crab
22 June to 23 July

Ruling planet: the Moon
Triplicity or element: water
Keywords: changeable, protective, loving, shrewd, caring
Lucky day: Monday

 LEO: The Lion
24 July to 23 August

Ruling planet: the Sun
Triplicity or element: fire
Keywords: generous, warm-hearted, proud, fun-loving, dignified
Lucky day: Sunday

 VIRGO: The Virgin
24 August to 23 September

Ruling planet: Mercury, the planet of communication
Triplicity or element: earth
Keywords: modest, shy, practical, intelligent, over-critical, perfectionist
Lucky day: Wednesday

LIBRA: The Scales
24 September to 23 October

Ruling planet: Venus, the planet of love
Triplicity or element: air
Keywords: balance, justice, harmony, partnership, sociability, refinement
Lucky day: Friday

 SCORPIO: The Scorpion
24 October to 22 November

Ruling planet: Mars, the Roman god of war, and Pluto, the god of the underworld
Triplicity or element: water
Keywords: intensity, depth, determination, jealousy
Lucky day: Tuesday

 SAGITTARIUS: The Archer
23 November to 21 December

Ruling planet: Jupiter, the planet of self-expansion
Triplicity or element: fire
Keywords: optimistic, freedom-loving, philosophical, expansive, honest
Lucky day: Thursday

 CAPRICORN: The Goat
22 December to 20 January

Ruling planet: Saturn, the planet of structure
Triplicity or element: earth
Keywords: cautious, reserved, prudent, ambitious, constructive, disciplined
Lucky day: Saturday

AQUARIUS: The Water-Bearer
21 January to 19 February

Ruling planet: Saturn, the planet of structure, and Uranus, the planet of disruption
Triplicity or element: air
Keywords: independent, intellectual, distant, idealistic
Lucky day: Saturday

PISCES: The Fishes
20 February to 20 March

Ruling planet: Jupiter, the planet of self-expansion, and Neptune, the planet of confusion
Triplicity or element: water
Keywords: emotional, sensitive, moody, imaginative, impressionable, changeable
Lucky day: Thursday

IF YOU ARE BORN ON THE CUSP

I can't begin to count the number of times I have had people tell me that they are not sure if they are a Gemini or a Cancerian, a Scorpio or a Sagittarian, because they were born on what is called 'the cusp'.

To me, this is unthinkable and I will often go out of my way to find out which sign the sun was in at the precise time that they were born. In different years the sun comes into the signs at slightly different times. Because it would take a newspaper or magazine too many pages to list all of the crossover dates for each sign over the last hundred years, they only print a general guide. There are many of you sneaky signs out there who just enjoy reading two horoscopes for the day and picking the one you prefer.

If you are one of those people who have spent the last seventeen or seventy years not knowing your sign, then find out today. It could make the difference between success and failure, and it will certainly explain some of your idiosyncrasies. If you are on or near a crossover date, then look it up on one of the many free astrological websites or log on to my website, www.claireshoroscope.com.

Part 1

LOVE

Chapter 1

LOVE OR LUST?

Most of us have been there. You're living your life as best you can when suddenly – *bang* – out of nowhere your eyes lock and you realize that someone has hit you like a bullet. You want to be with them and spend your time with them. You want to know everything about them; you want to inhale them and be them; you are in love. Or are you? How do you know if the person you fancy or the person you are with is the one for you?

Compatibility is a big part of any successful relationship, be it marriage, work, children or friendship. If you have any doubts about your compatibility, ask yourself if the other person is making you happy more than they are making you sad. If the bad times outweigh the good, then you know you have to make some changes. There is always a choice and always another route you can take. Dead ends do not exist, no matter how bleak the view.

We have all been guilty of following our hearts, and various other parts of our bodies, rather than our heads, but a real partner should be a best friend and lover rolled into one. It is no good *saying* you love someone. You have to *feel* it with your heart and soul. Some of us have even been guilty of going out with someone who looks good but isn't quite as shiny under the surface. Sex is an important part of a relationship but, as many of my older clients will tell you, it is certainly not the be-all and end-all. You need to be able to talk to the person you are with after your two minutes, two hours, two days or even two years of passion are over. So to find out if you are truly compatible, you have to answer the following questions honestly:

1. Do you love the person you are with – or even just fancy them if you are not going out with them – because they are popular or because they make you happy?
2. Have the good times when you have seen them or been with them outweighed the bad?
3. Would you trust this person to make the right choices with your best interests at heart?
4. Do they treat you in a manner that leads you to feel you are special and that you have something to offer to the world?

If you can answer 'Yes' to these questions, then you are already on to a winner. Now let's take a look at the different sign combinations.

If you fancy a fire sign

If you fancy a fire sign, Aries, Leo or Sagittarius, then you will probably initially have been attracted by their sense of humour and the way that they can make a joke out of any situation. They will have raised a smile, but can they keep that smile on your face? If you are a fellow fire sign, then you shouldn't have trouble understanding the way that they operate and you will in fact fall in step over the years so that eventually you walk to the same beat. If you are an air sign, Gemini, Libra or Aquarius, the more you get to know them the better you will be able to understand them. Your flirtation will continue to improve with age.

If you are an earth sign, Taurus, Virgo and Capricorn, or a water sign, Cancer, Scorpio and Pisces, the relationship will still function well, but you may have to work a little harder to understand why you both act the way you do. You will know if it is lust rather than love if their sense of humour starts to go. Fire signs can always laugh in a crisis, and if they no longer seem able to have fun, you would be better to let them go.

If you fancy an earth sign

Earth signs, Taurus, Virgo and Capricorn, are very sexy people indeed and you probably first noticed them by the way they walked and the way that they wore their clothes with just the right bit of flesh showing to turn you on. If you are an earth sign yourself or a water sign, Cancer, Scorpio or Pisces, then the sex will just get better and better and you will have the best of both worlds – love and lust. If you are a fire or air sign, then you need to make sure you don't change too much for the earth sign that you fancy. It is one thing to adapt but quite another to submit completely.

If you fancy an air sign

Air signs, Gemini, Libra and Aquarius, need someone with whom they can talk about anything and everything. They love fellow air signs and adore fire signs, Aries, Leo and Sagittarius. Nothing is too much trouble for them when they are together and within a few months of meeting they are usually hopping on a flight to somewhere different and exciting. Earth signs, Taurus, Virgo and Capricorn, can tend to play things a little too safe for air, but water signs Cancer and Scorpio and Pisceans actually walk too far on the wild side and have to work hard to find a happy medium.

If you fancy a water sign

Water signs, Cancer, Scorpio and Pisces, want love and lust together and can find it with their own element. They can find it with earth signs also, Taurus, Virgo and Capricorn; but air signs, Gemini, Libra and Aquarius, and fire signs, Aries, Leo and Sagittarius, can tend to be a little too independent for watery souls, who like to be in control in all manner of ways! I think the trick here would be letting these signs think they are in control – a skill that if learnt can make for a happy and fulfilled life for both parties. In fact I'm sure it's been the secret to many a happy marriage over the years.

Meeting someone who is compatible with us is one of the most wonderful experiences we can have. It affects us in so many ways. Some of us lose our appetite, especially the Scorpios and Virgos of the zodiac, while the Aries and Pisceans can't seem to stop scoffing once they're in love. There is rarely a better time than when Cupid first fires his arrow your way. Let's take a look at the different signs and how they act. You may just be able to uncover the tell-tale signs as to what your friends are really up to when they say they're working overtime! You can also learn how to recognize when you're in step or out of sync with a partner. This is a valuable key to reducing stress and to making sure that you're with the right partner and not the wrong one!

Aries

Should I stay or should I go?
The Ram is a sign that is passionate by nature and so when they embark on a new relationship, they tend to act like a love-struck teenager. No one else in the world will exist for them, and work falls by the wayside. They shouldn't try to lie to their boss by saying they're ill, though, for the truth will be obvious from the expressions on their face. They also seem to think more about what they're wearing when in the first throes of love. (Although I'm afraid to say that this does tend

to go out of the window three months down the line – sorry to disappoint you!)

They will want to know everything about you, even going so far as buying your family presents in order to soften them up for the exciting first meeting. Being ruled by Mars, the planet of unpredictability, you may want to check what they're wearing before you take them round to meet the family. They're likely to have gone overboard and you may have to tone down the very colourful display they've put on in your honour.

Before you know it, they'll be planning your life together. You'll catch them writing their name with yours on napkins, and I've even known a woman of this sign who was discussing with her brand-new partner how he would have to take her maiden name as his just didn't suit her Christian name. (In spite of this, they went on to get married and he did take her name!) My point is that they are a little tactless but in the nicest way, and what they are thinking while in this giddy, loved-up phase often tumbles out of their mouths. The good news is that they do slow their pace after about six weeks and so the drawer at your house that they claimed pretty much immediately will start to become less full and life will gradually become more manageable. In fact one of the complaints I often get from partners and ex-partners of this sign is that the Ram goes all out over the first few months and then backs off. As long as you know this early on, you will be less inclined to take it personally.

Money is not the most important thing to this sign, so you won't need to take them out to expensive restaurants. You may have to order takeaway, though, as when they first fall in love, they're not going to want to leave the bedroom for days if not weeks to come.

Signs that an Aries is not happy

A clue that the Ram is not happy is when they don't make up after an argument but simply sweep any issues that were being discussed under the carpet. Watch out – they haven't forgotten, they are simply simmering, and there is a cork that is about to burst in your direction if you don't tackle the contentious subject head on.

If you're an Aries who thinks they're having problems with their eyes but never did before, then take a love check not an eye test, as Aries rules the head and this sign often gets major headaches when under stress and pressure. You need to retain some independence and keep your own life ticking over. When you make major changes quickly, it can all too often lead to disaster. I know you don't want, to but you have to make changes a little more slowly if you are to achieve longevity with a partner.

I once had an Aries client who spent the first six months of a new relationship travelling around the world and staying at different top hotels with their partner. Luckily they could afford to do so, but I could have saved them a lot of hotel bills. Once the couple returned home and normality kicked in, they couldn't stand each other. The Aries began showing sides to their character that the Taurean involved couldn't live with. The unpredictability and excitement were all very well when in exotic places with new experiences, but back on home ground the rubbish wasn't getting put out and the food wasn't being put on the table, something the Taurean couldn't stand.

Learn to be yourself. Aries are known for being impulsive and you should explain to all new partners that you are an unpredictable and spontaneous sign. Don't try to pretend that underneath that almost shy and reserved air you are not a born leader who wants to decide at a moment's notice to change plans, and that for anyone to try to rein in your sense of adventure would be like asking you not to breathe.

Best place for a first date: comedy club, to find out if your date has as alternative a sense of humour as you do!

Key lesson for an Aries: slow down – if they love you, they're not going anywhere.

Taurus

Should I stay or should I go?

Now this is a sign that was born to love. Taureans are natural and instinctive lovers who will go out of their way to make a new partner feel cared for and appreciated. A somewhat alternative view of sex can produce a few raised eyebrows among the more conservative of signs, but don't worry – Taureans won't go too far.

It's hard for many people to see immediately that this sign finds them attractive, as they are deep thinkers who take time to come round and find the courage to put their heart on the line. Once you get them talking, you're sure to discover a sensual, loyal and affectionate person who will show you unparalleled sincerity.

The funny thing about Taureans is that they tend to become childlike when they are in love. I'm sure that this is something their loved ones find very funny indeed, for people of this sign are usually leaders and dominant. Even their voices can take on a childlike air, but this is simply their way of giving up the natural power of their sign to show that they like you and are making space for you to have a say in their life.

Be careful if you're a sociable sign, though, as you're not technically allowed to have any other friends in your life.

Now that you've found a Taurean, you have a best friend and a lover rolled into one. You've heard people say that some men want a woman who's a lady in public and something quite the opposite in the bedroom. Well, now you've found out who it is they were talking about. A Taurean will help you to take stock of your life, and you will probably find that you've never been better looked after and that your abode has never looked more like a home. The problem is that your Taurean will have neglected their own life in the process. If they say you can't come back to theirs, it's probably because they've spent all their time and energy on your place and so are embarrassed by the mess in their own home. It's unlikely any housework has been done since they met you! I once had a client who pretended to his partner that he was still going to work when really he was going down to the Job Centre as he had been sacked for not turning up at work during the first two weeks of their relationship.

Signs that a Taurean is not happy

A clue that a Taurean is unhappy is when they start to let themselves go and stop taking care of the things they usually take pride in. One of the good aspects of this sign is that they're not backward in coming forward. You won't need to ask twice if you've upset them. If their pet name for you is replaced by a less kindly one, then you know you've started on the downward spiral. This earth sign can be as bad as its polar opposite, Scorpio, when it comes to sticking the knife in, and indeed sometimes their words can cut to the bone.

The problem is that it's hard to talk them back round again once they've started falling out of love. It's taken them a long time to feel this way, you see; so if you really do love them, you're going to have to pull out all the stops to make it up to them.

Trust is the main issue for a Taurean, and if they can't trust you, then do them and yourself a favour and cut each other loose. If not, you may be like one of my clients who only discovered after his beloved wife had died that his severe upset stomachs were in fact down to the eye drops his long-suffering spouse regularly used to place in his evening meal. Ouch!

When in love, Taureans will turn their whole world upside down for you, so when they start to put friends before you, then you know that they're not truly happy. They do find it hard to talk about their problems, though, so at the first sign of strange behaviour make the effort to go for a walk and talk to them about life and how they're feeling. The trick with this sign is to catch them before things go too far. As long as you're still talking, then there is every reason to believe you can work things out.

Over- or under-eating is also a tell-tale sign that something isn't right in the relationship – unless the Taurean is in the first throes of love – so watch out for this confusing but revelatory signal.

Bless them – all they want is to be loved and to love you in return, so give them a break.

Best place for a first date: the nicest restaurant you know.
Key lesson for a Taurean: fear of failure will bring on failure. Let go and have faith.

Gemini

Should I stay or should I go?

After I've given a Gemini a reading, their friends often try to find out what's been said and tell me that their friend can't possibly be happy, because they've gone from being a carefree spirit to one who is penned in and is no longer seeing the lighter side of life. I just smile to myself and explain that the Gemini they know wasn't carefree at all but was in fact restless and unhappy, and has been waiting for someone to come along and help them stop playing games and simply settle down. What the Gemini's new love needs to understand is that no matter how much a Gemini wants to settle, and intends to do so, there will always be a gypsy in them who wants to explore life and live new adventures. The only difference now is that once the honeymoon phase is over, they've got a pal by their side to share their antics – if you can keep up, that is!

They won't like the characters in your life who tell you what to do, so beware and hide away anyone in your family who has strong opinions. Gemini won't hold back from telling them what they think and feel.

This is a sign that longs to have someone to take care of them. They are like a superstar who has finally come off-stage and can kick off their shoes and not worry about being seen without their make-up. This is because life really is like a performance to them. So if they've let you in, then you must be very special indeed. You may have a problem putting up with the vast array of characters they have in their life, but this is all part and parcel of what makes them such a magnetic sign. They have a charitable side to them, which I'm sure you will grow to love over the years you're with them.

Geminis can do more than one thing at once – this sign is the ultimate multitasker – so don't think they're being rude if they email or make phone calls while talking to you or even while in the throes of passion (yes, I mean it). They won't be neglecting you; this is what they're good at and they are quite capable of sealing a multi-million-pound deal while bringing their partner to a high-pitched squeal of delight!

Signs that a Gemini is not happy

It's a sure-fire thing that a Gemini is not happy when they are physically tired all the time. This is one of the signs whose health really is a mirror image of their emotional state. They also tend to become loners when in the midst of getting out of a relationship, which is an obvious clue that they're not being themselves. This is one of the most individual signs you will ever meet. Fun is the key to this their happiness. They were born to laugh and to socialize, and the minute they stop laughing, you know you've got trouble.

A Gemini's nightmare would be watching one of those couples you see who have been married for a long time and sit opposite each other in a bar or a restaurant with nothing to say. The couple may claim they don't need to talk, but a Gemini would beg to differ.

Make sure that you keep yourself looking good for this sign. Many people believe that once you're in love you don't need to keep trying, but you do with a Gemini. If they're no longer thinking about how they look, then they've stopped caring, and it's vital to their happiness that the attraction is kept up and that the excitement remains. It's when the excitement is over that this sign tends to stray. Yes, I know it can be exhausting trying to think up ways to keep a relationship alive and the spark strong, but many couples do it and a Gemini will accept no less from you.

If you can lead the conversation with a Gemini for more than five minutes, then you know that their mind is elsewhere. By that same token talking is this sign's saving grace. Ask what's wrong and they should tell you; they're far more upfront than Aries and Taurus in that way. Nerves often get the better of them, though, so becoming ill is often a sign for this usually bubbly personality that life is not as they like it.

Best place for a first date: an airport, and don't forget your passport!
Key lesson for a Gemini: it doesn't hurt to stop and take in the views of others once in a while.

Cancer

Should I stay or should I go?

This sign is so changeable in nature that it is hard at times for even the most astute of people to work them out! They are born carers who know how to make someone feel loved but whose feelings are often not reciprocated in the manner they should be.

Be honest with this sign and they will love you until the end of time. They are more than capable of taking on your troubles for you, but lie to them and they will never forgive you. They can't comprehend why, when they're willing to accept your past, you won't open up to them and tell them everything. Some people would say they are a little cold, but that's not true; they just want the facts and they want them now.

It's true they don't forgive, but as far as they're concerned, they can't and shouldn't have to tolerate a lie. They are faithful and supportive and have been the support system for many a successful man and woman who has risen to the top.

Don't expect them to fit in with your friends. It is impossible to expect that they get along with everyone you know. You can also guarantee that you'll have at least one friend who will ask you what on earth you're doing with such a sign, as some would label them as nutty as a fruitcake. The way you've got to look at it is that fruitcakes are delicious and delectable even if they need careful handling. And what fun! Just don't give them too much to drink. This sign is not known for taking alcohol well and will be liable to say things they don't mean.

You certainly won't find a more original sign when it comes to Christmas or birthdays. In fact they go overboard. Don't try to second-guess what they want from their relationship with you. They'll constantly surprise you and will always make life interesting. Respect is a key ingredient for getting along with this sign and is what will help keep you together too. Their friends mean a lot to them, so if you want to impress them, then be nice to their nearest and dearest. It could end up being a vote-off between you both if you insult a loved one or put them down, and if they've known their friends longer, you may well end up with the short straw!

Signs that a Cancerian is not happy

You can tell a Cancerian is feeling the strain when they start to attack. Just like a crab, when they decide to fight they go all out. Whoever said attack is the best form of defence must have been talking about a Cancerian. They don't cope very well with long-term problems, and if something doesn't get fixed quickly, they can fall into a depression from which they can take weeks if not months to recover.

Their stubbornness is their own worst enemy and, like their polar opposite, Capricorn, can often be an unnecessary reason for the breakdown of a relationship. If you love them and want to keep them, then back down because they're certainly not going to!

This is probably the sign that is most obviously affected by the moon and tides. When there is a full moon, you'd better run for cover, and if a Cancerian looks at their diary, then they're likely to see it was during a full moon that they broke up with an ex or gave in their notice at work.

Health-wise, when this sign gets down it's hard to lift them up again, and they need constant care, love and attention to make sure they stay on the right track in life. Relationship problems affect them more than most. They are not as good as other signs at forgetting things that have been said or at sweeping wrongdoings under the carpet.

The other problem is that they often talk to their nearest and dearest about their problems before you. If Auntie Jane or Uncle Mick is giving you funny looks, it's probably because they know you're going to be chucked! If you've made a Cancerian feel inadequate or hurt, then they will try to cover things over with a smile, but look into their eyes and you'll see whether the smile is hiding heartache.

In some ways they're like a child – full of innocence and hope for the future. What's wrong with this, though? Surely to have a sign that is so full of genuine and lovable traits should be an asset. The time you spend placating and reassuring them will be returned tenfold, so make the effort. Words of comfort and reassurance can work miracles.

Best place for a first date: at their home, so they can see if and how you fit into their surroundings. (If they even let you in the front door, you know you're off to a good start!)
Key lesson for a Cancerian: don't expect. Allow a blank canvas with no preconceptions.

Leo

Should I stay or should I go?
They don't mean to, but this is a sign that really can't help acting on impulse. They are not frightened of the kind of experiences that the rest of the zodiac would run a mile to escape. Born initiators and leaders, they take partners to new heights and push the boundaries, making life fun and fresh for all around them. However, their intense attitude can make a relationship with a Leo a little scary. After all, who wants to talk about wedding plans when you don't even know if their favourite drink is tea, coffee or wine? Such minor details don't put off a Leo. What you must know is that after the first six months they back off and they probably won't even remember asking you what song you wanted to be played on your wedding day. They will, however, remember how to

make you laugh. In fact it's their humour that will keep the rest of the signs coming back into their life year after year.

The problems begin when a Leo falls for a partner who is as impulsive as they are. That's when you need to take care that you don't end up at a drive-through wedding chapel!

With their magnetic personalities and ardent natures, they are usually very attractive both physically and mentally. They also have a tremendous affinity with the younger generation, for this is truly a sign that is young at heart. Watch out, though, for it is a determined sign and I've witnessed many a client unsuccessfully try to fight off a Leo's attentions. It's their sheer determination that often sees a partner capitulating. That teamed with the charm that this sign naturally possesses is a sure-fire recipe for a dramatic and memorable relationship.

Keep a sense of humour at all times – you'll need it. You'll probably never have as much fun with anyone as with this sign. And don't worry about their flirting, by the way; they can't help it, and if they love you, they're probably telling those they're flirting with how much they care for you.

They love to tease, which is why they're so irresistible. This really is a case of the chase being every bit as sweet as your wildest dreams could imagine!

Signs that a Leo is not happy

When this larger-than-life character no longer has a smile on their face, you know that trouble is coming. Depression in a sign such as this often affects them physically. The calm before the storm is an uneasy time and you'd best run for cover to ensure damage limitation.

Money problems can affect a Leo's personal life more than most signs. Because Leos are such proud characters and like to be able to treat those around them, they find it hard when they can't afford to do so. Any gathering or party appears to be theirs even if it's not. They command a room without effort and want all eyes to be on them. This is why it has such a catastrophic effect when things aren't working out. Feeling humiliated because something isn't working is devastating for this sign, and they have been known to go to extreme lengths in order to try and cover up problems.

If you ever find out that a Leo has been cheating, then be glad that is the only fallout you've experienced, as Leos wouldn't cheat unless they weren't happy. They would rather show their dissatisfaction through actions than words. It's part of their animal make-up that they don't see the need for trivial talks and discussions. They will force both your hand and theirs by making a situation impossible to ignore.

This sign can't bear to be controlled, so be wary of telling them what they can and cannot do or of giving them too many limitations in life. Remember that a Leo is a born explorer and to be told they can't do something is like giving them permission to be bad!

If you stop taking care of yourself, then they will lose interest and stop taking care of you, because they think that the people they love should always make the effort for them. If you see things starting to go wrong between you, don't wait to sort them out. Leave it a night and it could be a lifetime before you get the chance to win them back. Deal with problems as soon as they happen and talk things through. They respect honesty but can't tolerate a liar. Having said that, they're allowed to tell white lies when required. To them, a white lie is simply adding colour to a story, and who'd dare to argue with this delectable and very colourful sign?

Best place for a first date: somewhere loud and colourful, so you can let them know you're not afraid of a bit of drama.

Key lesson for a Leo: let others take the lead; it's sure to prove more interesting.

Virgo

Should I stay or should I go?

Once you have a Virgo in your life, you won't have need for a personal secretary, a best friend or a parent, for you have all three rolled into one. Some may say they're boring, but others find it a turn-on to get a text or an email telling them when and how they're next going to have sex. While some signs are flirting with the idea of seduction, Virgo will have it planned right down to the colour of bed linen you'll be lying on afterwards!

The beauty of this sign is that they will take your life, dissect it, work out where you are going wrong and instantly make improvements. OK, so you may not have planned on having a life make-over, but you won't be able to deny that your life is better for having this sign in it.

With their competence, quick thinking and compassion, Virgo can make you feel loved as never before. They enjoy life and are able to adapt to situations that many other signs in the zodiac could not.

Some would say that this sign is boring, but I disagree emphatically. Flirting with wild ideas is exciting enough, but here you actually have a sign who is willing to carry them out. Talk about pushing the boundaries!

Virgo spends a lot of time counselling friends and family, so you are going to have to be prepared to share this loving sign. It isn't unheard of for a Virgo to take phone calls while in the throes of passion as their role of listener is of paramount importance, even in the most intimate of moments. This sign probably celebrated when earpieces came out for phones as it made them immediately available to the many friends who can't live without their advice – or so Virgo seems to think.

Don't take it personally if they dissect your performance in the bedroom. They're only trying to help and will probably be able to improve your skills. They're not necessarily experienced, but they've talked to so many people that their tips are probably worth picking up!

Don't make the mistake of thinking they are unhappy with you if they are moody or acting strangely. They find it hard to compartmentalize so it could just be down to a bad day at the office – it isn't necessarily anything to do with you.

Signs that a Virgo is not happy

A Virgo is clearly unhappy when they go off into a dream world and pretend that a situation is diversely different from the way it really is. I once had a client who became so embarrassed when he separated from his wife that he lied to his family and told them there was nothing wrong. He went so far as to leave things of his wife's about when his family came round and told them that she'd just popped out to the shops. He simply couldn't admit that his marriage had failed. Of course his family found out in the end and he is now happily married to a real person again. They should have guessed when he said she'd popped out shopping, for Virgo would never let anyone go shopping without them in case they bought the wrong thing!

Although exciting, Virgo is a very draining sign to be with. Don't think that they don't know exactly what they're doing, as they will have planned their seduction of you, from how many children you'll have to looking up your family tree on the Internet to make sure the breeding line is up to the standards they require. If they don't want you, then it won't take a scholar to work out that they're not interested any more. This is a sign whose emotions are written on their face, and they will drop you faster than a hot brick if you're no longer showing your affection for them.

Best place for a first date: let's be honest here – let them decide. They've probably already got a table booked somewhere anyway!

Key lesson for a Virgo: don't judge others on who they were before they met you.

Libra

Should I stay or should I go?

Life with this sign is a mixture of highs and lows. You may be scared off at first, but think about it – what's more fun than living with such an extreme array of emotions? It depends on your own sign and how seriously you take this fun-loving character.

Librans are natural flirts. They just can't help it. The flirting is not about trying to win hearts; it's about having fun. They don't even flirt to get people to like them. They just love life and the fun that comes with simply being here on earth.

When it's time for the serious stuff such as paying bills and day-to-day living, they can be somewhat unpredictable. They have an eye for beautiful things and so may be prone to spoiling you with gifts. All very well until you find out a month later that your present has been charged to you own credit card!

It's not part of their make-up to want to hurt you; in fact they'd go out of their way to make sure they didn't. They just can't seem to help acting on their emotions rather than with their brains, which means that inevitably they don't always make the best choices. They feel their way through life and love, and wouldn't be with you if they didn't utterly adore you.

They know, thanks to their ruling planet, Venus, how to get what they want, and even though they themselves often suffer from emotional blackmail, they also know how to use it to their advantage.

So what, you may ask, do they want from you? Your complete attention and devotion is the answer, even though they probably won't be able to give you theirs. They are attracted to age differences, usually going for someone older as they want to be with someone who can teach them things. Ever the explorer and researcher, life is for learning and making more beautiful. Not only will this sign build a life with you, they will decorate it too!

Signs that a Libran is not happy

It's not easy to spot when this sign is unhappy as the Libran character is made up of so many layers that it can take a while to find out what they are really thinking and feeling. When they fall for the wrong type of person, they can go a long way down the wrong path before they find the strength, courage or fortitude to do something about it.

Those Librans who have been severely hurt in love take on physical problems as well as emotional ones; it really is as if they have had their heart broken and it's a very sorry sight to see. They are not the easiest sign to help, so once you see the tell-tale signs and the puppy-dog eyes, help them to help themselves. This loving sign thrives when in love and is an extremist. Then again, being ruled by Venus, the planet of love, would you expect anything less?

There are often hidden meanings to their words. They inadvertently give clues. If a Libran's prepared something different for dinner when you sit down to eat together, then start asking questions. Their emotions are revealed in their actions and this could well be their way of telling you they want something from you.

If a Libran starts to insult your family, then you really know it's over. After all, this sign loves the unity and closeness that family ties bring. I have seen even the worst family legal scenarios be worked out thanks to the support of a Libran. So when they no longer support your difficult parent and start knocking down your familiar walls of support, then you know that the gloves are well and truly off.

Oh, and if you already have your suspicions that your Libran love has strayed, then watch and see if they're still flirting with the person concerned. If they are, then you know you're safe. The chase is the best bit to them, so if they're still flirting with someone, they haven't conquered them.

Best place for a first date: somewhere they can appreciate true beauty and art. A work of art or a city by night, the choice is yours.

Key lesson for a Libran: be yourself; don't act the way an ex would have wanted you to.

Scorpio

Should I stay or should I go?

I don't know why people ask me if they should stay with a Scorpio or leave them. You see, you don't actually get a choice. A Scorpio does the deciding, not their partner. They are great at being in charge but letting you think that you are. This intense, determined and at times very jealous sign will keep you interested throughout your life. I have even known clients who had a teenage relationship with a Scorpio being unable to resist checking up on their ex year after year in order to find out what this dramatic sign has been up to.

Friends are important to them, but unlike some of the signs, family has always and will always come first to the Scorpio. Blood is most certainly thicker than water, and when they are feeling happy and confident, they can make really major changes in their lives. I have had Scorpio clients over the years who have altered their lives beyond recognition, and this is because they don't see the same limitations that many of the other signs do.

The right partner is not just important to them, it is essential. Love is what helps them to breathe. You may think from your experience with them that they are thoughtful and intense, but I call it wise. They watch, wait and learn, and that's why their moves seem so dramatic when they make them. They've planned everything down to what outfit and shoes they're going to wear for the showdown.

Love and hate can come very close together for this sign. They do everything in their life with such intensity that it can often be hard to tell the two emotions apart. Love Scorpio and they will go to the ends of the earth for you. They'll even up sticks and move wherever you want. Making dramatic changes is the norm for them, but don't think they'd do this for anybody or just for the excitement. They have to be in love with you even to take a step in your direction.

You see, Scorpio doesn't suffer fools gladly and is likely to have a small, select group of friends rather than a crowd. They may not talk about the past but that's not a conscious choice. To Scorpio, life probably didn't exist before you came along, not in their mind anyway.

Signs that a Scorpio is not happy

A Scorpio is not happy when, like their sign of the Scorpion, they sting and ruin lives and say things that hurt. Why? Because when a Scorpion stings it is the last resort, so they really will have been pushed too far.

Whatever you do, don't cheat on this sign and expect to get away with it. You may be sitting pretty thinking dumb old Scorpio never found out about the fling you had, but you'll soon realize that they do know and probably followed and photographed every moment of your indiscretion, which they'll post on the Internet for your friends and family to see. They actually knew you were thinking of straying even before you did. Look again at the fine food you are being served and ask yourself why you've not felt right of late. Look deeper still and you'll find the detergent that's been put in your food drop by drop every day. Revenge is a dish best served cold to this unforgettable sign.

A friend of mine who is a Scorpio used to say to her children, 'Don't even think about it!' The horrified children would gather in their room to ask how on earth she'd guessed what they were up to before they'd even finalized their naughty plans. Scorpio just knows!

Although a very sexual sign, they cannot give love freely if their heart is not in it, or at least their libido. That's why if a Scorpio is no longer accepting your amorous advances, you know that they no longer feel the same way about you. They have to be in love with you or very much in lust, and be able to trust you if they are to give themselves to you. It's all in the eyes with this sign too. They may not show it in the way they stand or the things they say, but the eyes really are the windows to this sign's soul. If they can no longer make you eye contact when they look at you, then you know there is something bubbling under that cool, calm exterior.

Talking is important to them and if you stop talking and communicating, then they will shut down on you too. They need to know what you're thinking and feeling every step of the way. They want to share the experience with you, and to shut them out of your life is like shutting off their life-support system.

Such a powerful entity is the Scorpio that when they enter your life, you'll feel as if you didn't know what it was to live before; but if their feelings wane, then you'll never have known such pain. Be true to them and avoid lies and they'll respect you. This is certainly not a union to be entered into lightly, but it is one that will change your perspective on life for ever.

Best place for a first date: your home, so Scorpio can investigate, save themselves time and find out *everything* about you.

Key lesson for a Scorpio: you don't have to reveal your whole life story on the first date.

Sagittarius

Should I stay or should I go?

When things are good, you will probably never have been happier, but when they are bad, you will wonder how you got into the very flamboyant world of the Archer.

Part of the problem is that while some of the other signs may want to consume you and be with you twenty-four seven, Sagittarians can find it hard to give themselves to you completely and so part of you is always going to be wondering what your union really means. There is no real reason for this; it's just part of their make-up. They have one foot out of every situation in case they need to make a quick getaway. This isn't always due to a past experience with an ex; it's just in the nature of a fire sign to have an escape route ready and waiting in case the alarm goes off.

It's not unusual for this sign to have boxes in the attic that they haven't unpacked even though they moved years ago. They're so busy hurrying on to the next thing that they sometimes fail to finish what they've already started. That said, this really is a highly successful sign who can excel at whatever they put their mind to, if in fact they can put their mind to any one thing.

Their saving grace is their common sense, which tends to kick in just in the nick of time. They can take a normally diffident sign of the zodiac and help them to excel and make their mark in life. They don't tire as easily as many other signs, so while some of us are packing our bags and giving up on a relationship or a dream, a Sagittarian is getting their second wind.

Their way with words is another fantastic quality. I have watched friends being talked back from the brink of ending a relationship and start planning their wedding the very next day. You have to admit that is a talent worth its weight in gold. This strong sign can draw you into their world and make life such a special place that nothing else and no one else matters. The Archer has a charisma likened to celebrity. It's no wonder so many of their partners feel lucky to be with them; they believe they've landed a saint!

Signs that a Sagittarian is not happy

When they tell you so! This is an honest sign who doesn't have time to play guessing games. They'll sit you down and get straight to the point, and could save the rest of the zodiac a lot of time with their tips on speaking frankly.

When predictability and routine become the norm, then you can start counting down the days to their exit. Surprise them with loving gestures and thoughtful actions and you'll keep this sign by your side until the end of time. Don't expect to retire where you live now, though; Sagittarians rarely stay in one town for too long!

Life with a Sagittarian can be heaven and hell combined. One minute you've planned a future and the next they're telling you that you're not part of it. Their impulsive nature can deter others from telling the truth as they serve their opinion as cold as ice and straight to the heart.

You will notice that this sign is naturally quite healthy, so clues that problems are coming can be spotted when they start to catch everything that is going. Believe me, a Sagittarian doesn't make a good patient. So rare is it for them to get ill that they act as if the common cold is the plague.

If you love this sign and want to keep them, then be as straight with them as they are with you. It can be all too easy to tell this sign what you think they want to hear for fear of letting them down. However, not all of us operate at the same velocity as the Archer, so slow your pace and make them follow your lead every now and then. It can do them the world of good to take in the view instead of acting as if everything in life is a competition.

They would rather be broke than live with a liar, so tell it like it is to keep this sign. They can forgive even the worst of sins if told straight, something that often shocks the more conventional signs in the zodiac.

Best place for a first date: their work; it's sure to give you an insight into the mad empire they run!
Key lesson for a Sagittarian: don't pretend to like things you don't just to impress others. Be your own person.

Capricorn

Should I stay or should I go?
It is not easy for a Capricorn to commit themselves in love, so if you have managed to attract this very sensual sign into your life, then you have done very well indeed. They are cautious by nature and it can take an eternity for them to commit to the most trivial of things, let alone something as major as a relationship.

When I'm in a queue and the person in front of me is taking their time, I often joke that they must be a Capricorn and I'm usually right. It's for a good reason, though, and they can save their friends and family a fortune by informing them how much they could have saved by buying two of such and such, or by getting a larger size of an item.

This sensible approach doesn't follow through in the bedroom, though, for this is one earth sign who knows how to make their partner feel at home. In fact it's probably the home many of us have been looking for, as a Capricorn can make you feel as if they've known you for your whole life and bring a uniqueness to many unions.

Their sense of humour deserves a mention, as they can say something with a straight face but on the inside they know that they're joking with you and it can take hours if not days for outsiders to get the real joke.

The more in love a Capricorn is, the younger they seem to appear. It's as if love is a wonder drug. I have a Capricorn friend who regularly has Botox and also has many men friends. When I see her looking well, I have to check whether it's because she has a new man or has simply had a shot of Botox! A truly happy Capricorn won't need any help from a needle, though; an injection of romance is all they need to make everything else in their life slot into place. They may have said they were happy as a singleton, but when you see this sign as part of a couple, it's a truly amazing sight. They do need to stop treating their partners as if they were a prize or a trophy, though. They can't help it; they're proud and probably in shock that anyone could find their very specific ways work well for someone else too!

Signs that a Capricorn is not happy

There are no half-measures with this sign. Home is where the heart is, and if their heart is no longer with you, then their time and energy will no longer be where you are either. With the strong likes and dislikes this sign has, your phone number will be deleted within the week, and if you've done something to hurt or upset them, then they will probably have already arranged for your number to be barred too.

They don't want a humdrum existence; they have standards to keep, and if you can't keep up with what they want, then they see no reason to waste any more of their precious time. This is where their very individual sense of humour comes into play again and their ex is sure to be the butt of all their best jokes. If you are placed outside their circle, then you can expect to find yourself on their list of funniest things to say.

It's not that Capricorn is lazy. It's just that they very often start new relationships before old ones are properly tied up and put out to pasture. If there is a nearly ex still on the scene, it's probably not actually Capricorn's fault. They're just a little slow in getting to the point when trying to finalize things.

A word of warning if you think there's something going wrong in your relationship with Capricorn: check your bank balance! Earth signs value their money and their possessions, and I once had a Capricorn client who suspected his relationship wasn't going to work out. Before he even attempted to fix the problems between himself and his partner, he drained all their joint bank accounts as back-up in case things didn't work out. This was more important to him than talking things through. So check your joint account as you may be in for a shock. Your balance may tell you whether you can expect to find your Capricorn partner there when you get home.

Best place for a first date: an impressive place with impressive service. With the right service, ambience and decoration, they'll be putty in your hands.

Key lesson for a Capricorn: don't be afraid to be yourself. Avoid saying you don't know.

Aquarius

Should I stay or should I go?

If you manage to get a word in edgeways with this excitable sign, then you will soon discover that they already know more about you than you think. You see, an Aquarian will not enter into a union without having done their homework first. To them, it's essential to make the round of phone calls to find out where you've been, what you're doing and where people think you're headed in life.

You have to forgive the Aquarian, though, as they can't see they're doing anything wrong. Great at social networking, they are able to get the kind of information out of people that others can only dream of.

The good news is that if you're with an Aquarian, you can be sure it's because they *want* to be with you. This is not an easy sign to hold on to, as their flirtatious nature means they often find a relationship is hard work. If they are with the wrong person, it can make them feel tied down. That's why they don't commit unless they think you could be 'the one'.

They are good judges of character, which is another reason why embarking on a romantic relationship means they really do believe you can make it work. Just try not to dredge up too much about their past. They believe that life is about the future and not about going over old ground. They grow bored talking about what has been and would much rather work on what could be. This forward-thinking, ambitious and very fun sign can make any situation enjoyable.

If they make plans that don't involve you, then don't get paranoid and think it's over. This is a sign who can have a life and a lover. They don't need to be handcuffed to you to love you. They have a wide social circle, and if you want them to want you, then let them be free. They go where the wind takes them, which is where there is choice and laughter. They have a point: life should be fun, and if trust is present in the relationship, then there is no reason not to give them the benefit of the doubt.

They will change their plans and even move towns and countries for you if they think it would make you happy, which many of the other signs would not. All you have to do is keep the fun and sparkle in their life, as this is the very air that they breathe!

Signs that an Aquarian is not happy

When the laughter stops. It won't stop for long, though, as they need to be able to smile. They are naturally happy people who don't enjoy looking at life's negatives. They won't run out on you when the chips are down; they'll help you move onwards and upwards, but they expect you to remember that the glass is always half full, never half empty.

Many problems occur for this sign when the partner they are with becomes lacking in self-confidence and thinks that they are not good enough for popular old Aquarius. The truth is that an Aquarian will never pick the type of partner that others would choose. They go for the outsider, someone they believe to be out of their league. They see the potential in people and can turn an average character into a superstar by the time they've built up their confidence.

Don't forget that although this is a forward-thinking sign, it is also a fixed sign and so has some very traditional values. Stick to the promises and plans you've made or you could find yourself exiting the next phase of your union, rather than entering it.

Others may say that Aquarians are easygoing, but those who live with this lovable character will know that's not true. You've heard of people who moan about partners who squeeze the toothpaste tube in the middle or can't stand it when their loved ones don't close the lid on the washing-up bottle. Well, they were talking about Aquarians!

If you stop taking care of your physical appearance, then your Aquarian will lose interest. It's not that they are shallow; it's the opposite in fact, as this is one sign for whom a mental and physical attraction really does go hand in hand. You have to seduce this sign's mind as well as their body, as they go for the whole package. Hard work, you're absolutely right, but worth the effort, I can assure you.

Variety is the spice of life to this sign, and if they're stuck in a rut, then you will be too. Arrange a night out or book some train or plane tickets; the rewards are sure to be worth every penny!

Best place for a first date: an eclectic music mix while cooking in the kitchen. (Remember to put the lids back on the ingredients as you go!)
Key lesson for an Aquarian: don't make promises you can't keep. Enjoy today without wishing for tomorrow.

Pisces

Should I stay or should I go?
Never enter into a union with a Piscean lightly, for your life will never be the same again. I mean this in the most fabulous way you can imagine, and I mean in a way that you will never, ever forget. This emotional, impressionable and sensitive sign will add colour to your life and ignite your interest in completely new areas and subjects. Even the way you look at yourself, your family and your future will take on new meaning.

They will love you unconditionally and take on your faults

as if they were their own. They don't mind baggage; they handle it better than most when in the mood, and worse than most when feeling out of control.

Pisceans work well as a team, for they throw themselves into a situation with more strength and gusto than many of us have seen in a lifetime. They have an instinctive knowledge and know what to do to make things right.

They are unselfish to a fault and won't think twice about taking on things that other signs would run a mile from. Here's where the catch comes in, though, as they will expect you to love them back in return and they will notice the minute, the second that your feelings begin to wane. It's a hard union for anyone because it's so mentally and physically exhausting, but for those of us who enjoy the highs and lows of life, it also offers a buzz that proves truly addictive.

It could take you ten lifetimes to work out what makes a Piscean tick and even then you wouldn't have every question answered. Don't expect them to tell you everything that's gone on in their lives, though. It is rare to meet a Piscean who doesn't have some sort of secret hidden in their past. Because they are such dramatic characters, their secrets can range from a past marriage to simply lying about the price of a piece of clothing they own.

You can be married to this sign for sixty years and still not understand them, but that's often why their marriages last so long. With the trust issue out of the way, there's room for mystery and excitement, something that helps many of the signs feel truly alive. To come home and find out you're off on holiday for the weekend instead of to the supermarket would not be uncommon when living with this sign, but with their ambition and drive they'll support you and can help you realize your wildest dreams and desires.

If you stay with them and work things out, then you will be unbreakable, but if you do decide to part ways, then you can be sure that your dalliance with them will go on to shape every single relationship you will have. They place as much importance on little things as they do on big things. This is where problems can begin, as it can be as important to them that you commit to the holiday of their choice this year as the marriage contract.

I had a client who made his marriage with a Piscean last years longer than anybody had ever expected. When I asked him the secret to his happiness, he simply smiled and revealed, 'I let her think she's in control.' This is a really interesting concept and could, I believe, be a major key in making a union with this larger-than-life character go the distance.

Signs that a Piscean is not happy

If you go to hold their hand and they pull away, you know you've got problems. This sign needs to have lots of genuine affection if they are to give themselves fully sexually. Otherwise they can be all talk. I have known two people of this sign who planned weddings to other signs of the zodiac and didn't go through with them on the day. Even though they'd put all that work and expense into their big day, they weren't prepared to go through with something they weren't 100 per cent sure about. Luckily one of the weddings went ahead a month later, but only when the Piscean had the answers and reassurance she needed. It cost an absolute fortune for the couple, but she didn't care. She had her man the way she wanted him and walked down the aisle with a positive mind. A Virgo would not have dared plan a wedding unless they were sure, and they certainly wouldn't have cancelled it at such short notice, but be prepared to have your cheque book ready when making up with a Piscean; you're probably going to need it!

Be true to this sign and give them your heart and your

commitment. That's all they want – to know you won't embarrass them and that you will support them and be by their side. Their life takes such unexpected turns that they can't afford to have their co-pilot hit the ejector button when they don't expect it.

Best place for a first date: delving through your old photo albums. They want to know where you've been and what they're getting.

Key lesson for a Piscean: don't get to know them through what others think of them.

Meeting

Where are you most likely to find each sign of the zodiac, though? Want to mix with your own, or just learn where the sign of your dreams can be found? Read on to discover where the confident ones of your sign hang out.

Aries

Jump on a course for inventors, go to a seminar for setting up your own business or find out who else is patenting a new design. Expect to see Aries composer Andrew Lloyd Webber or fashion designer Vivienne Westwood, and maybe even an Aries soulmate too.

Taurus

Any good restaurant, or perhaps eating the starter in one, the main in another and dessert somewhere else. Bump into

Taureans Jack Nicholson, George Clooney and chef Gary Rhodes for a sight and night to remember.

Gemini

Working in a social place or just hanging out, even during the week, as they can't stand to be alone for long. Expect to get served by Gemini types such as ad man Charles Saatchi and Gemini singer Kylie Minogue.

Cancer

Campaigning for some great charity. Expect to find Cancerian Richard Branson there too and turn an ordinary night into an incredible one. Life will never be the same for you again once you've mixed with this magical sign.

Leo

Wherever is the showiest, most over-the-top, extravagant place to be, with an outfit to match of course, and looking great. Think Leos Geri Halliwell and Madonna. Spice up your life and you'll soon be getting into the groove.

Virgo

While sorting out the glass and paper at your local recycling centre, expect to bump into a Virgo, who'll be taking care of the environment and making sure everyone else is all right. Virgo Sir Richard Attenborough did this for people and animals alike.

Libra

Poetry readings and places of inspiration and gorgeousness. Libran T. S. Eliot won hearts with his words, and Librans will do the same for you.

Scorpio

Simply stand outside a stage door or hang out where the actors go and you'll expect to see Scorpios such as Whoopi Goldberg, Danny DeVito and Goldie Hawn. Bring the curtains down in spectacular style with a Scorpio.

Sagittarius

At the local sports centre but hanging out as much as working out. They're known for their great figures, especially the legs, such as Sagittarian Tina Turner, though they don't need a lot of work to stay looking on top form. Fly high and reach for the stars.

Capricorn

Out walking the dog. The irresistible Capricorn has even been known to look like their pet. I bet Capricorn Nicholas Cage has no shortage of offers from dog walkers when he's out and about.

Aquarius

Down at a comedy club or anywhere that has humour on offer, the drier the better. You're likely to find a 'friend' like Aquarian Jennifer Aniston hanging out there. Take things a step further and discover the magic that is an Aquarian.

Pisces

The latest art showing. Beauty and architecture are irresistible to this sign. Michelangelo was a perfect Piscean as his work in the Sistine Chapel testifies. Create beautiful art and music with this beguiling sign.

Secret Hangouts

Let's take a look at where the twelve signs would go but wouldn't want to be found. By understanding that we're all allowed a little room for mistakes, we can forgive each other's foibles.

Aries

The racetrack, where they just know their horse will come in this time.

Taurus

The takeaway, before they go home for their dinner.

Gemini

One more pub or coffee shop on the way home, for a final social.

Cancer

Shopping with the credit card they swore they'd cut up.

Leo

Out with the friend they hate and swore they'd never be seen with again.

Virgo

Sidling up to an ex, agreeing how they've both moved on.

Libra

Buying tickets, which they'll claim they've been given by a friend for free.

Scorpio

Buying more of what they've already got.

Sagittarius

At the place they said, but not for the very important business meeting they insisted was taking place.

Capricorn

Flirting with that new face at work to see how far they'll be allowed to go.

Aquarius

Writing cheeky texts and emails too good not to send.

Pisces

Going to places they know they can goad an ex or even just the new competition.

Chapter 2

LET'S STAY TOGETHER

Understanding how your sign tends to behave when in a relationship can boost your confidence when you are faced with the kinds of problems life inevitably throws your way. It's OK to feel nervous about a relationship and to question what you want, but it's also good to trust and to move forward.

Aries

All too often you have rushed into unions and have been left feeling as if you have taken on more than you wanted. When these nerves kick in, you tend to blame those closest to you for tricking you into a situation you didn't ask for. The only problem is, you did ask for it – insisted on it, in fact! The key to confidence in relationships for your sign is to take things more slowly. You may say that it's others who are rushing you, but stop and take stock and you'll soon realize it was *you* who initiated every change.

Believe in the power of patience. Have faith in your loved ones and listen to them. You frequently tell them what they're thinking and feeling before they've had a chance so much as to open their mouths. You're very good at finding humour in situations and you must use this ability in order to laugh at things that go wrong. I had an Aries client who called off her wedding the night before because she was frightened she had rushed into things. She was so good at finding humour that she even talked her husband-to-be into having a 'not-married' party at the venue, which had already been paid for. Luckily the groom in question was a Gemini and had no intention of turning down a social opportunity such as this.

Key word to learn: patience.

Taurus

Many clients I have had of this sign have stayed and stayed and stayed in a negative relationship, for the children, the dog, the house, the material things . . . the list really is endless. What is clear when talking to these clients is that something else is always given as a reason to stay. The truth is that 50 per cent of the time Taureans can be too lazy to leave. You see, emotionally they've put so much of themselves into a relationship that they're not entirely sure they've got the strength to go through what it would take to get out!

Talking is the key for you, Taurus. You all too often bury emotions, which in turn makes you physically ill. One doctor friend of mine actually asks his patients what sign they are when faced with a mystery illness. If he's dealing with a Taurean, then 70 per cent of the time he believes that it's emotional stress causing the physical problem.

You have to learn to accept the fact that not everyone will do things your way and agree to have some 'me' time so that you don't get driven crazy by not having things done exactly the way you want them. If you've got a more dominant partner, this can often be the case. Communication counts for everything.

Key word to learn: talk

Gemini

We all know by now that you are a social animal and like to flirt when you get the chance, but if we look at the other side of the coin, we see that you are also a very private creature when you choose to be. Close ones may think they know what's going on in your mind, but you still manage to surprise them. I actually had a married Gemini client who managed to form another relationship, put a deposit down on a house and get engaged before her husband even had a clue what was going on.

The popularity of your sign is the reason for the very dramatic life you lead. You get opportunities that many of us can only dream of and you have a charismatic quality, which means you will have supporters and admirers waiting in the wings should current faces let you down. However, with your sign it's always a case of believing that the grass is greener and that you have to keep up with the Joneses. You must learn to appreciate what you do have before you start complaining about what you lack. You also need to stop looking for compliments and start giving them out to your loved ones. No one would choose to be with your sign if they didn't love you, so appreciation and a bit of commitment are what you need to learn if you are to achieve a permanent, and not just temporary, buzz in life.

Key word to learn: value.

Cancer

It's hard for you Cancerians to believe what you're told by your loved ones as you're emotionally scarred from birth – you can't quite believe your mother put you through such a traumatic journey! There is a small part of you that believes the world owes you. This is not quite as harsh as others may think. From early on in life you give your heart and soul to all you meet, so of course you're going to be crushed and hurt by those who don't do the same in return. While other signs have flirtations, every contact that you have is a relationship that has touched you to the very core of your being.

The only problem is that you often miss out on the fun that normal, day-to-day experiences can bring, as you're far too busy looking for those highs and lows. You don't really understand normality and have been known to make a change just for the sake of it. I've had clients of your sign who have left their partners because they were bored. When I asked why, it was because he or she just sat there and watched TV or because all they did together was the school run and cooking dinner. To you, this is not the norm. It's only when you experience a divorce or a major break-up that you go looking for the very qualities you threw away!

Key word to learn: faith.

Leo

You very attractive Leos have spent your life being told how great you are and if one person happens to tell you that you aren't so great, then you go on to believe this for years to come, no matter how hard new faces try to repair the damage. People will look at you and see someone who is confident, but they need to know that any arrogance you exhibit is purely there to conceal the fact that inside you are terrified that someone won't like you any more, or that they'll discover you're not as intelligent as they thought you were. You are clever and very lovable; it's just that you constantly raise the stakes for both yourself and those close to you. You're like an athlete who's run a huge distance but won't believe you're great until you've beaten your personal best.

You need to learn that it's OK to let others take the lead and that allowing someone else to choose the restaurant or arrange a night out doesn't have to be a recipe for disaster. You also need to know that you don't have to be held accountable for your family's mistakes. Being born under this sign, you think that you have to take on the world's problems, whereas all loved ones want is to see you relax, something that's not easy for any fire sign.

Key word to learn: acceptance.

Virgo

If you didn't set up the meeting, make the first approach or decide to take things to the next level, then there are likely to be problems. You don't want to be in control – in fact you'd love nothing more than to leave others to do all the work – it's just that you don't trust anyone! One of the main problems you experience in life is that you can't stand not knowing what's going to happen next. If you could know what your close ones were going to say in advance, you'd be as happy as Larry.

You are often attracted to the type of person friends and family would never choose for you. You see, you like people for what goes on in their mind and not just the superficial face that they present to the world. You expect others to be loyal to you, but you also want them to put you before anyone else. You're not used to being second best, and the real reason for this is because you lack the confidence to believe you're worthy of them. Poor thing, you don't believe you're an asset to anyone. You need to have faith in yourself, and others need to learn to bend a little more. It's like asking someone to take a rollercoaster ride for the first time – you're petrified and need talking to, along with support and love. Fear of the unknown can cause you to leave a relationship, but trust and courage can make incredible things happen.

Key word to learn: flexibility.

Libra

Yours is a sign that often falls in love far too quickly because the idea of love appeals to you more than the reality of the situation. Close ones should not worry if they hear you talking about an ex with love. It's not the ex you're remembering; it's the picture of them you built up in your mind. If you have found the right partner, there's no way you'd willingly let them go. Your loyalty is fierce and your love undying. If you do get out, it really is because it isn't working. You expect relationships to shape up immediately and don't let partners know what is wrong.

How can someone fix something if they don't know what's wrong, though? Emotional blackmail is something that you are all too often subjected to. You want to please your loved ones, but find it hard to know how far is too far and so you end up doing things that you wouldn't otherwise have done. I had a Libran client who was unhappy with the pet name her partner had called her for forty years. It took a visit from me for her to resolve this bone of contention, which she was about to leave him over. You Librans must learn to feel with both your head and your heart, and never with your libido. It is only by doing this that you will find your world to be a fair and just place.

Key word to learn: patience.

Scorpio

Yours is a sign of such extremes that it would be hard *not* to know when you are feeling happy or sad. The problems begin when you start going into self-destruct and hurting yourself because you have been hurt. This destructive behaviour can range from giving up on your career to under-eating and over-eating. Loved ones know when you are happy, though, for you will have an inner confidence that others won't be able to help but comment on. By that same token, if you are with the wrong person, others will be able to tell. They wouldn't dare tell you, though, as they know you'd bite their head off.

Having said that, you Scorpios can do a very good job of pretending to be happy when you're not, because you can't stand the thought of ridicule or of the world finding out that you made the wrong decision. If you could stop living your life as if it were a soap opera and start to enjoy day-to-day things, then you would soon relax. You are always looking for the next drama, but the problem is that not all dramas are constructive. You should try to get this sort of excitement from other areas, such as your career, so that your loved ones don't have to continually check to see if they're in or out of the doghouse.

Key word to learn: enjoy.

Sagittarius

Because your career is often so very important to you, it's hard for your loved ones not to feel as if they've been placed second. Even if you are in a career that doesn't pay a lot of money, it's still your vocation and you expect your nearest and dearest to respect that. If you don't have a career, then you'll definitely have a hobby that one day may be a career, and once again your loved ones have to bow down to this and accept that they come second.

When you want to, you can make your close ones feel incredibly loved and wanted. Yours is a sign that holds the power to make others feel safe. You were born wise and know more than most because you understand that the world is a tough place. Because of this, you set out in life ready to tackle anything that might come your way. Your heart is not so strong, though, and it's only by giving time to love affairs that you learn to trust, no matter how loyal a sign you have chosen to be with. People can never quite work your sign out and that's because life is a continual learning process for you and so you're never ready to let anyone settle on a firm summation of you – not for a long time anyhow!

Key word to learn: mellow.

Capricorn

You Capricorns love your friends and families, and if your partners can't get on with your loved ones, then they may as well head for the door now. If there's a best friend they can't abide or an auntie who rubs them up the wrong way, then they should call a truce as they're going to need them in their corner at some point in their relationship with you turbulent Capricorns.

For some reason yours is a sign who is always looking over your shoulder. You feel like you're on the run even though you probably haven't done anything wrong (most of the time). There is something smouldering about your sign (think Kate Moss) that cries out to be cared for, but you won't let others too near. You know when you meet someone famous who has a presence about them? Well, this is the normal

Capricorn. You have something about you that others just can't put their finger on but which is irresistible. The danger comes when you feel that close ones' loyalty has strayed and so you look elsewhere. With the number of friends you have, you won't find it hard to keep yourself busy somewhere else. The problem for you, Capricorn, is that you're like a kid in a sweetshop, but who needs a bar of cheap chocolate when you could have one quality square? Prioritize and enjoy life should be your new motto.

Key word to learn: relax.

Aquarius

It's all too easy for you to believe that you've done exactly what close ones wanted when in fact you've done precisely what *you* wanted. You speak but don't always listen, and it can be hard for you to see things from others' point of view. That said, you are a great visionary, but it's usually your dreams and ambitions that you've shaped so perfectly. You ignore advice and do things your way. You are a great leader, though, and by understanding the mood of a nation or the feel of an era you can bring much pleasure into the world. Think songwriter and singer Aquarian Robbie Williams: he tuned in to the nation's changing mood to have hit after hit, but in his love life he has never been able to understand what works for him. All too often relationships end up like oil and water. The answer is to keep both feet in your relationship and stop having one foot out. It can do neither party any good if there is only one of you in a relationship most of the time.

Key word to learn: listen.

Pisces

You have this fear about life, as if you're going to fail in what you do no matter how hard you work. You see, you have always lived through hardship in some form. It's not surprising because you live life at such a fast and dramatic speed. You have people whom you have known and loved and admired, and you also have people whom you have hated but still admire. You are a complicated and fascinating sign who is sure to heavily influence the life of everyone you touch. Once someone falls in love with you, they will never again experience life in the same way. You change the way others perceive the world because you see things through such an alternative view.

Your need to live life to excess and overdo things must be addressed. If you can focus this energy positively, then you can have a successful career and a happy family, and what's more you'll do it with style. Your problems come when you lose respect for your mate, which happens when you're let down. Learning to address a problem before it escalates is a core ingredient to success.

Key word to learn: breathe.

Jealousy

I'm going to end this chapter with a short section on jealousy, a very human emotion but one that can easily threaten a relationship. Some signs are more jealous than others. Water signs, Cancer, Scorpio or Pisces, feel that the people in their life belong to them and them alone. Sometimes they don't even like to think about their close ones having a best friend apart from them, let alone anything more. Earth signs, Taurus, Virgo and Capricorn, are actually real home bodies and don't like to have their personal lives invaded unless it is by invitation. Sometimes even if you give them a month's notice that you will be going out without them or having people round, they can become jealous and lose control.

Whatever sign we are, in this day and age we often spend more time with the people we work with than with those at home. This can lead loved ones to feel as if they're second choice, even if they're not. That's why communication is important, so that we feel secure enough to have it all: a good job, a happy family, the right circle of friends. There will be times when we can't be at home as much as we want, and it's important we have a secure base for when we can be there. Trust is essential.

Air signs, Gemini, Libra and Aquarius, are a little more laid back than the rest of the zodiac. This is because they are more open to social aspects than the other signs, not to mention the fact that they enjoy flirting! They tend to know more often than not that if someone close is talking to another, it does not necessarily mean that they fancy them.

I have to say that a little bit of jealousy every now and then never did anyone any harm. What about that friend who has bought the very outfit that you had your eye on last week but weren't able to get your hands on? Half of you is hoping that they don't look as good in it as you would, aren't you? Well, that kind of jealousy really is at the bottom of the scale and isn't anything to worry about. It's when you begin throwing darts at pictures of your partner's new workmate that you need to start questioning if your emotions are a little out of line.

The first step to finding out how jealous you are is to ask yourself if the real reason you don't like a person is because they are taking a close one's attention away from you. The next question has to be, is what they want to do any real danger to what you have together? Is the life and the relationship you built up changing? If it is, then you may need to sit down and work out a strategy so that you approach your partner in the right tone and manner. If you're not careful, your insecurities can be the factor that breaks you up.

If your partner is a fire sign, Aries, Leo or Sagittarius, then they do tend to go through phases when they want to explore new areas or faces. It means they're bored, so you would be best to lead their attention away from what they are doing by keeping your spirits up and talking about new things you can do together. Don't accuse them outwardly as it was probably a fire sign who invented the saying that the best form of defence is attack, and you'll only find yourself worse off.

If your partner is an earth sign, Taurus, Virgo or Capricorn, then you first need to question what may be wrong in the home. A move or even a more orderly home may be required. Your partner may well be seeking security elsewhere. I am not saying that this is a fact, just a possibility and a way for you to test things out.

If your partner is an air sign – that's Gemini, Libra or Aquarius – and is making you rage with jealousy, then whatever you do don't try to put a stop to their socializing. This sign loves people and hates their own company. Your first stop has to be, if you can't beat 'em, join 'em. Get your glad rags on and show them that you too can mix and mingle should you so desire. They'll soon be dragging you back home for some of your undivided attention.

And last but not least water signs do, I'm afraid, get a kick out of making people jealous. If a Cancerian, Scorpio or Piscean doesn't have at least one person who is jealous of them, then they don't feel alive. This is usually because underneath they are slightly jealous of the face concerned.

Don't indulge in games with these water signs, though, or you'll end up in a stalemate. They are a determined bunch, but wouldn't be with a partner if they didn't really love them. Sit them down and talk to them face to face; you will be able to read their thoughts in their eyes.

If a relationship is meant to work, then it will. If your fate is sealed in the stars, then so it shall be, but whatever sign you are born under don't be frightened to talk about how you feel. If you don't do this, then you will never be able to feel happy and be yourself. If something is so fragile that it is easily broken, then it was never working properly in the first place. Be strong and move on to better times.

Chapter 3

WHEN THINGS GO WRONG

Some of us will admit a relationship is not going to work within five minutes of meeting, but others will need to experience every level of joy and pain before we consider parting ways. Admitting that things aren't working is all about being honest with yourself about what and who makes you happy. It's no use pretending you can live a life that is not you just because it looks good from where others are standing. No one is perfect, but each of us deserves to acknowledge what we need. The first step is the hardest, but knowing that there is always a tomorrow can help you to find the honesty and humour to leave the past behind and embark on a new future.

Cheating

It is never easy when we find out that someone has cheated on us. It can leave us in a mess. Often we are too quick, whatever our sign, to blame ourselves. The reasons behind infidelity are numerous. Geminis often think the grass is greener on the other side of the fence and want to know what they are missing. Scorpios and Pisceans cannot resist their emotions or their physical needs, while Aries, Leos and Sagittarians all too often just act on pure impulse.

Although earth signs, Taurus, Virgo and Capricorn, are the least likely signs in the zodiac to cheat, they can do if circumstances push them in this direction. However, these three signs hate to break up a home, as their base is one of the most important things to them, the one constant that makes the rest of their life work.

Whether or not you forgive an affair is up to you, and different star signs handle betrayal differently. Water signs, which are Cancer, Scorpio and Pisces, find it hard, if not almost impossible to forgive. You see, they wear their heart on their sleeve and you might as well hit them as betray them. It hurts them both physically and mentally. Earth signs, which are Taurus, Virgo and Capricorn, worry more about other people than themselves in any time of crisis and do tend to find themselves dealing with an issue later rather than sooner. Of course, a delayed reaction can cause numerous other problems and they need to try being as honest with themselves as they would like others to be with them. Air signs, which are Gemini, Libra and Aquarius, just have to talk about what has happened, and counselling or a good friend who is willing to listen is essential to their road to recovery.

Just remember that whatever sign you are, only you can decide what you can or cannot live with. Every sign has its good points, and every sign has its bad points. You know what you can forgive and what you can't. Always remember that honesty may be dearly bought but can never be a penny badly spent. Don't pretend something isn't happening. You'll only make it worse for yourself in the long run. Bring anything that is bothering you out into the open or you will never find the tomorrow you are searching for.

I know many clients who have forgiven affairs and continued on to have a good life with the man or woman they share it with. I also know many others who could not forgive and who split up. Life is what you make it, and sometimes Taureans, Virgos and Capricorns tend to stay in a situation for the sake of their family, all the while making themselves more and more unhappy. There is always another sunrise, and there is always another choice, so sit down and work out what you want and not what suits others. If friends don't support you in your decisions, then they are not your true friends. Go on and find some friends who will let you live your own life and help rather than hinder you.

I Love You Darling, But . . .

OK, so you now realize that the relationship isn't working, but what should you do about getting out of it? Many water signs, Pisces, Cancer and Scorpio, will probably reach for the bottle and aim to get drunk in order to gain the confidence to announce their imminent departure, while Virgos and Librans will have a far more concise plan that has been written down with diagrams and time schedules (along with a 'who owns what' section of course). Here are a few tips for the most painless way to get out of a relationship that just isn't working any more.

Aries

Write down how you feel before saying it. Show it to a friend you know and trust and ask them to write a better version of what they know you are trying to say. A sense of humour is not appreciated at this point, so resist making that all-too-easy joke on exit, please.

Taurus

Don't start telling the person concerned how well they've done out of you because you've spent x, y and z over the last month and they have spent nothing. You're ruled by Venus, so put their feelings first and tell them how much you care for them before giving them a bill for their half of the meals you've eaten together over the last ten years!

Gemini

Many exes of Geminis find out they've become an ex when they meet or catch their beloved in the arms of their new love. Resist the temptation to start new relationships until you've finished the old. And remember, if you become friends with an ex, it doesn't mean you can go on sleeping with them!

Cancer

It takes you a long time to come to the point where you admit something is not working, and then you can be as cold as ice. Try to show some compassion and bear in mind that an ex doesn't have to be an enemy. Remember the good times and promise to part with a smile. It will mean a lot to you later.

Leo

If they've stopped treating you well, then you don't want to be anywhere near them. Lack of respect is the number-one reason for this sign to leave someone. Your partner should be able to tell by the power-dressing you do that you're there to break up with them. Learn to talk and not shout. I know you want to hear their side of the story before you leave.

Virgo

You've been planning this right down to the perfume you'll wear when you walk out of the door. Just remember that no one is perfect and a person's foibles are all part of their make-up. Too many Virgos want to get back together with their ex the next day, so make sure you're doing what feels right to you and not what looks right to others.

Libra

If they don't show you love, then you can't show them respect. Pride is important to you and it takes you a long time to get over a break-up. Relationships become a part of who you are, so you can all too often lose sight of yourself as an individual. Talk to the person concerned in the same way you talk to their friends, who can't fill in the missing blanks with the same honesty and clarity.

Scorpio

You'll be all out for the person who has upset you and they'd be well advised to cross the road if they see you coming. Calm down and count to ten. The truth is, you're better off without them if it's not working. You'd only end up slowly torturing them if you stayed.

Sagittarius

You may not even bother to tell them personally that you're leaving. Your sign has been known to do so by fax or email. Have the heart to at least make a phone call. You'll feel more at peace with yourself if you do.

Capricorn

You'll talk about what went wrong until the end of time, as you want to be sure there was no way you could have worked things out. You'll also be tempted to go back and give it another go if the person concerned is any good at emotional blackmail. Writing down pros and cons is perfect for your sign.

Aquarius

You'll have told all of their friends before you get round to telling them, and you're actually very good at humiliating an ex too. Leave with pride and tell them to their face; you'll feel far more like a grown-up if you do.

Pisces

You may have had professional counselling to decide this. You may have spent days confiding in friends, or – like one client of mine – you may, have drained the joint bank accounts before you informed them. Either way, it's like being hit by a train when you leave. Word of advice: play fair. Your reputation precedes you, my friend.

Getting over a broken heart

Whether you were the one who was dumped or whether breaking up was your idea, the end of a relationship can still be very painful. If you're finding it hard to move on, try these top tips for your sign.

Aries

Embark on something you've always wanted to do but have never done because of your ex-partner, whether it's a trip somewhere they wouldn't visit or a hobby or interest you placed to one side since being with them.

Taurus

Dress for yourself again, and start to enjoy the personal pleasures of music and entertainment that make you happy, rather than what fitted in with your ex's tastes.

Gemini

Call up the friends you dumped for your partner. With your effervescence and passion for life, they'll be glad to have your company again.

Cancer

Spend time with family and talk about the past and your loved ones without fear you're boring anyone. A perfect partner for you will not mind if you talk about things that they have not been a part of; they will encourage it.

Leo

You can have a career and ambitions again without worrying that you are threatening your relationship. Make this the time when you go for the career you had put to the back of your mind. With your insatiable appetite for success, you're sure to pip others to the post.

Virgo

Say what you want to without fear of being judged harshly for your opinions. Move on to a better future by being you again. You all too often shape your opinions based on what you think a loved one wants to hear.

Libra

Enjoy some time on your own and take any lessons you have learnt as something constructive. You have to be able to acknowledge and let go in order to move on. Talk to someone, a friend or a professional, and you'll find you become a better person and partner for it.

Scorpio

Write down your feelings and experiences, but don't go back to a bad relationship. All too often your sign returns to give things 'one last try'. You would not think about leaving if you were happy. Make new plans that are bigger and better than ever before. With your luck you'll pull them off if you focus.

Sagittarius

Don't feel you have to prove what a good time you're having as a single by staying out late at all the popular hotspots. This is an obvious and bad choice for you. Instead enjoy the normality that comes from not having to try so hard. The natural and relaxed you will instantly attract a better life and a better partner.

Capricorn

Further education and picking up on something you enjoyed but left behind for a partner will give you joy. Your sign never stops learning and loves travel. Mix the two together and put the spark back in your life and eventually it will be in your heart too.

Aquarius

Talk about what you want and don't spend ages blaming yourself for all that went wrong in the relationship. You're great at focusing on the future, so use this talent to put a bad experience behind you by knowing and accepting what and who didn't work. Do this and what you need for the future will become clear.

Pisces

Don't drag yourself down further by way of punishment. Wallowing will only make you feel worse. Turn a bad experience into a great one by proving that you now know what you don't need. Don't be tempted to punish yourself; instead reward yourself for getting out of a situation that was not working by making better choices and putting yourself first, which all too often you have failed to do when in a relationship.

Ex-Directory

Ever heard your partner say or do the following? This is why you should be pleased you're not with your ex any more!

Aries

MAN: Always knows a short cut even though it takes you miles out of your way.
WOMAN: Can't wait to tell you a secret.
BOTH: Act first, think later.

Taurus

MAN: Is always right. His is the only way.
WOMAN: Has no sense of time.
BOTH: Are hopeless at repeating jokes or messages.

Gemini

MAN: A little backward in coming forward. You can lead him but never drive him.
WOMAN: Happier with a safety pin than a needle and thread.
BOTH: Need a gun to get them up in the morning, or to go to bed at night.

Cancer

MAN: Over-considerate, like when you're halfway across a crowded restaurant and he calls out to tell you where the loo is.

WOMAN: Won't leave the house unless every hair and eyelash is in place.
BOTH: Take too long over every detail.

Leo

MAN: Thinks nothing of telling your friend how much you paid for your new coat.
WOMAN: Excessively house-proud and over-protective.
BOTH: Must have the last word.

Virgo

MAN: Is very punctual, but can't understand others aren't the same.
WOMAN: Waits until you're miles from home before she remembers she's left the cat in the oven.
BOTH: Can't help doodling.

Libra

MAN: Always tells you what a mess you look, after you've left the house.
WOMAN: Just can't help flirting.
BOTH: Are great critics.

Scorpio

MAN: Can't keep his hands off his tie.
WOMAN: Asks what you'd like for tea and then serves something completely different.
BOTH: Are clumsy and erratic.

Sagittarius

MAN: Thinks nothing of bringing friends home when you're not prepared.
WOMAN: Spends all the housekeeping money on things she didn't want.
BOTH: Are manic finger-tappers.

Capricorn

MAN: Can make popping out for a minute last two hours.
WOMAN: Is always wise after the event.
BOTH: Are back-seat drivers.

Aquarius

MAN: Tells white lies as often as he takes a breath.
WOMAN: Always takes a suggestion as a promise.
BOTH: Talk too much.

Pisces

MAN: Can't help the nervous action of pulling or scratching his nose.
WOMAN: Uses chairs and floor as a wardrobe.
BOTH: Never bother with a coaster when there's a clean surface waiting to be ruined.

Part 2

FAMILY

Chapter 4

STAR BABIES

Is your Katie or Kim destined to be the next Kylie? Are you giving Liam football lessons when he should be getting singing lessons? Let's find out what life plan the stars have in store for your offspring while you've still got time to guide them in the right direction.

Aries

Imagine having a child such as Elton John or Diana Ross running around your home. You're sure to have realized the very day that you brought your baby back from the hospital that this little bundle of joy was different, and you'd be right, as those babies born under the sign of the Ram are all ruled by Mars, the planet of change and unpredictability, and they will do what they want when they want, so get ready for a life that, with these folks in it, is sure to be interesting, to say the least. Princess Eugenie is an Aries, and Fergie and Andrew are certain to have found their royal offspring coming out with some very dry humour indeed. Her sign is hot and explosive, and has great physical courage. Eugenie may have her mother's red hair, but she'd still be the fiery type even if she didn't. They want to make a difference in the world, and I'm sure Eugenie will in years to come.

The Aries baby

Most Aries babies like to have noise around them, so if you've been creeping around your Aries angel, then stop and put on some loud music instead; you're sure to see them tapping on the side of the cot in no time. They don't like their own company and will scream the house down if you dare to put them in a room on their own. In fact they will sleep far better if you set up their cot in the front room, where they can be sure they're not missing anything. These babies look more delicate than most, but believe me, as you'll soon discover for yourself, they're not!

The five-year-old Aries

This child will have perfected more than a few bad habits by this age and they have a tendency to rebel more than most against cleanliness and good manners. Don't worry, though, as this is a stage and is unlikely to last for long. It is a test to see how far they can go. You would be best to ignore these antics; anything that they know gets attention can become a device that they pull out as and when they need. Tantrums come and go, but don't usually last too long and this really is a vital time for them, so set the ground rules now and not later.

The eleven-year-old Aries

The more artistic side of their nature is coming out at this time, as is their sensitivity. Many Aries children join theatre groups or beg their parents to send them to stage school. They learn much now by becoming an agony aunt to friends and are sure to know all of the latest gossip. This is a role that will continue with them for the rest of their lives. They are quick to learn at this age and, if put in contact with the right teachers, their brain can see them at the top of their class.

The sixteen-year-old Aries

At this age they are really being pulled into artistic professions and many teen stars are born under the sign of the Ram, such as Victoria Beckham, who joined the Spice Girls to train for fame when most girls her age were thinking about getting a Saturday job. Those who do pursue the arts do well, but they need to make sure that they keep their feet on the ground. Too much energy and early success can fire off the rocket but doesn't make for an easy landing! If you want to support them, then just remember to be persistent. This sign doesn't always listen first time round.

Taurus

Watch out, Mums and Dads, for you could well have a William Shakespeare under your roof if you have a child born under the sign of Taurus! On the downside you might also have a forty-year-old living with you in years to come, as this is a sign who loves their family and their home and will probably be one of the last signs in the zodiac to want to set up home on their own. If they do, then they will probably still bring back their washing for you or pop round for food every week, even if they are married. They need their kin to feel happy and loved, and for some reason bringing home their dirty laundry makes them think you feel cared for!

The Taurean baby

Taurean babies can be demanding and have irregular sleep patterns. They seem to want a lot more attention than other star signs, but this is only because they want to be sure that you love them. They want and need lots of cuddles. Amazingly enough, though, by three months old this is a child who literally overnight turns into a little angel. Once they learn the art of walking, which can take longer than most, they will get their noses into anything and everything, particularly the kitchen cupboards and anywhere with food!

The five-year-old Taurean
This is a child who is impulsive, inquisitive and full of initiative. They are also really stubborn and if they decide that they don't want to go somewhere or do something, then you will have to enlist the help of at least a couple of family members to pry their fingers away from the door frame. You will be surprised at the way they develop and their achievements at school. They are not afraid to put their time and energy into their projects, even at this tender age!

The eleven-year-old Taurean
The biggest problem encountered in their education at this age is if they don't like their teacher. So if you have noticed that they excel in any area, make sure that they are happy with the way that their teacher is developing it. Pushing little Bobby's love of computers could well see him becoming the next Bill Gates if you play your cards right! Their personality begins to develop around this time and their independent nature becomes much more evident. They love music and should be encouraged in their fantasies, as these stand a stronger chance of becoming reality than you may think of.

The sixteen-year-old Taurean
They now have magnetic sex appeal. They won't really have a very high opinion of the opposite sex, though, and can be callous in the extreme, but they will attract admirers like moths to a flame. By now you will have realized that this is a teenager who knows they command respect, even if they do have their own somewhat strange ways. You can be sure that leaders in life such as Taureans Eva Peron and even ex-prime minister Tony Blair knew that it wasn't a run-of-the-mill life

that was in the stars for them. Taureans make the best singers in the zodiac, so don't mock them when they start telling you they are going to be the next winner on *Pop Idol*. Just look at famous Taurean singers such as Barbra Streisand, Engelbert Humperdinck, Bono, Bobby Darin and Janet Jackson. Get your cash out and buy them the train ticket; it's sure to be an investment that will keep you in clover for many years to come, especially as the Bull will always take care of their own!

Gemini

You'll need to be ready for anything with a child like this in the house, but you can also be sure that life will be entertaining. Don't be surprised if this child is an early talker. They have plenty to say and won't mind joining in with adult conversations. Not that they always make sense, though; in fact some would say the older they get, the more rubbish they talk, but it still keeps partners and loved ones coming back for more, time after time after time.

The Gemini baby

This is a most individual baby. Some mothers of these children do tend to worry that Gemini Georgie prefers playing with cars rather than dolls or that Gemini George wants to trade his train set for his sister's Barbie, but don't fret. They are just covering all bases and need to make sure that the grass is not greener on the other side.

The five-year-old Gemini

They enjoy ripping up paper and books, so don't leave your favourite novel lying around or you'll never get to find out the ending. These kids are daydreamers, and their eyes are usually a really distinctive feature. Even without talking they will be able to relay their feelings with those eyes. You will be able to take them to most adult functions without worrying that they will misbehave, and they tend to get on better with older children. Don't expect their educational reports to be fantastic. There is some way to go yet before teachers realize just what an individual they are dealing with.

The eleven-year-old Gemini

This is a child who should start to show a love of the arts, and this is probably the time when Gemini star Kylie Minogue took aim with her ambitions. They are starting to learn more and more from people now instead of from things. They love new experiences and will learn and pick up new skills quicker than most. They are not liars at this age, but they certainly know how to stretch the truth. You can hear them coming a mile off, as I'm sure Gemini Paul McCartney's mum can remember about her famous Beatle son!

The sixteen-year-old Gemini

You will be amazed at how much energy your child exerts at this age, as they can work two jobs, do their schoolwork and still find time to sneak into the local disco. By now they are more independent than ever and won't like being told what time to come home. They will not necessarily show great interest in the opposite sex, but they are attracted to characters and personalities. Friends are likely to be really varied as they try to take elements from each person to help them along their path in life.

Cancer

You have a really caring child here, but do bear in mind that you also have a very emotional one, as their ruling planet is the moon. When the moon is full, you may want to run for cover, because quite honestly anything can and quite often will happen. Most children of this sign have round faces and can turn on the waterworks and make you feel like the worst parent in the world. However, this is a child who learns the fine art of emotional blackmail surprisingly early and is very good at it too. This sign has an affinity with water and will probably even end up living near it. If they don't, they should, as it will keep them sane in times of trouble.

The Cancerian baby

This is a beautiful but rather fussy child, although well behaved with it – until the age of three, when they gain a bit more confidence and adopt a somewhat cheeky and pushy attitude. Do not turn your back on this child for long; here is a baby who could escape the clutches of an armed guard. Don't waste your money on expensive toys either: this is one infant who will have more fun playing with a tin of soup than a toy.

The five-year-old Cancerian

This child cannot be conned. You would think they have been on this planet before, they are so wise and clever. In fact at the age of five they may be a little too wily for their own good. From time to time they will go off into a world of their own, but they have a lot to think about, so give them space when they need it. Their shrewd business sense has already kicked in by now and they will want to know the pros and cons of everything. The 'why?' phase will be particularly trying with this child.

The eleven-year-old Cancerian

They are sure to shock and please you at this age, as they are surprisingly self-sufficient. Even if they get stuck with their schoolwork, they will endeavour first of all to find a solution on their own before seeking your advice. It is the deep and very thoughtful nature of this sign that makes them so worthy of the label 'wise', and is also why they can often appear much older than their age.

The sixteen-year-old Cancerian

I think I can safely say you now have the kind of teenager any parent would love to have. By now they have more often than not experienced a broken heart as they treat everything and everyone really seriously. They exude a kind of sexiness, which will probably cause quite a bit of stress for you. Just imagine how Cancerian Pamela Anderson's parents must have felt letting their sixteen-year-old *Baywatch* babe out with her mates! But all in all you have a character that is sure to be an asset to any parent's life.

Leo

Dylan Michael Douglas, son of Catherine Zeta-Jones and Michael Douglas, won't have any problems growing up with famous parents. Leos are born show-offs and leaders, although they are unlikely to want to go into their parents' professions. They are pioneers, just like Leo Louise Brown, the world's first test-tube baby! What you will find with this fire sign is that they are a little erratic with their behaviour and energy levels. One minute they can be talking ten to the dozen, and the next they can be as quiet as a mouse. This is due to the fact that they put their all into everything and so often have to take time out to refuel, as friends and family are sure to discover for themselves.

The Leo baby

This is a baby any mother would be proud of. They very quickly show off all of the skills and qualities that their loved ones could hope for. Alertness and intelligence often reveal themselves within weeks of birth. They are willing to amuse themselves for longer than most babies. They love attention too, though, and once they start talking, they find it hard to stop.

The five-year-old Leo

Your child will by now be full of energy and raring to go. Don't be surprised if they creep into your bed at 1 a.m. with an array of books for you to read to them. Don't even think about force-feeding them; they will let you know what they want, and as long as you can wait out this somewhat difficult phase, then you will have a loving child who will while away their time singing songs they have made up.

The eleven-year-old Leo

Poor old Madonna's dad must have had his hands full with this eleven-year-old living under his roof. When your child tells you that they want singing lessons or football lessons, or whatever their passion may be, you should get your wallet out, for they're certain to repay you ten times over when they turn it into a vocation. They will also remember your support or lack of it, so bear this in mind when the half-an-hour journey to a football match is becoming a chore! It won't be a hardship in ten years' time when you're making longer journeys by private jet while drinking champagne!

The sixteen-year-old Leo

It's hard to stop this child from talking, and they won't always say the right thing. They are not afraid of hard work or of working for a low wage if they know it will lead to the job of their dreams.

Virgo

This is the perfectionist of the zodiac who wants things their way or not at all. I mean, just imagine poor old Liam Gallagher's mum trying to force-feed him brown bread instead of white and think of his reaction! Children of this sign also have a tendency to be hypochondriacs. They are really good at listening to friends' problems, but will want their home run as they like it from nine years old, if not younger. They will decide what you do and when you do it, and no matter how much you swear that you are the boss, I'm afraid you're fighting a losing battle. The advantage is that this child will actually enhance your life, as if they don't like that new face you have introduced them to, there is usually a very valid reason, so back them up. They deserve it.

The Virgo baby

This is a baby who usually starts out in life looking more like their father and taking on their mother's temperament and personality. Virgos are actually not the most patient of babies, and even a minor job such as heating up their milk will take seconds too long for their liking. After the first four months any tantrums and crying should stop and you will be left with a baby that is weighing up your every move. Keep them occupied or they will catnap during the day and keep you up most of the night.

The five-year-old Virgo

You should now start to see the determination that is associated with this sign. If you don't start to get their number, they will have you over a barrel for the next twenty years, so make sure you put plenty of time and energy into this phase. Virgo Prince Harry is sure to have kicked up a right royal stink if he wasn't watched closely. In fact you can tell even now just from the twinkle in his eye!

The eleven-year-old Virgo

This child will make it clear that they don't mind not being the leader and are more than happy to take on the role of second in command. They can be a bit of a teacher's pet around this time and are more mature than most children of their age. They won't like going to school in dirty clothes or with loose buttons, so make sure you play the role of parent well or they may end up reporting you to social services!

The sixteen-year-old Virgo

They are still the golden child and give off a very sensible air, but what Mum and Dad don't know can't hurt them as far as they're concerned. They won't mind doing things themselves that they would be quick to reproach others for. Vanity and self-indulgence are their main downfall, but are also easily avoided. This is one teenager who's not afraid to take their education further.

Libra

Libran babies really do look as if butter wouldn't melt in their mouths. Just look at Leo Madonna's daughter, Lourdes, the image of innocence but with a strong will. Libran babies love to play devil's advocate, and if you say black, then they will say white. Don't think that Guy Ritchie has developed those frown lines on his forehead for nothing. If you have a Libran child, then just make sure you say 'no' and mean it when embroiled in a heated discussion with them. If not, you'll have them reasoning with you until dawn, and you'll probably end up losing, if they are typical of their sign.

The Libran baby

The Libran baby will coo and sing to you like the perfect child and you'll have visitors galore to admire your seemingly cute baby. Not so cute when you want to go to bed, though, for this sociable baby is not the best sleeper, I'm afraid, preferring to catch up on their sleep when the rest of us need to start our day! They don't mind playing on their own, but their downfall is their lack of confidence, which only their parents will be able to help them overcome. It is important that you encourage them as much as possible.

The five-year-old Libran

At five years of age this child becomes strong-willed and moody, and they have an opinion on everything. Don't even think about force-feeding them; you'll be wasting your time and theirs. It is easy for them to single out a member of the family to make their special friend. They do this with the intention of having influence on their side should Dad or Granny be thinking about not letting them have that new Barbie or football kit they've seen.

The eleven-year-old Libran

These are alert kids with quick wit and are musical by nature, so don't be surprised if they join the school choir. This child is sure to excel in one special subject at this age and more often than not it is art. They don't like to be told what to do, though, so their school report is bound to tell you that they frequently go off on a tangent. They are the class clowns and have plenty of friends, but they also tend to notice the opposite sex a little earlier than most.

The sixteen-year-old Libran

The teenage Libran usually adores their mum, and with their gift of the gab you are sure to feel as if you are talking to a